STOP STOPPING YOUR SUCCESS

A GUIDED JOURNAL TO HELP IDENTIFY AND CORRECT THE
NEGATIVE THOUGHTS THAT HOLD YOU BACK FROM SUCCESS

HARRIET M. HARRIS, MBA

Disclaimer: This guided journal is not a substitute for therapy.
The information within is not intended to guarantee success in
any way. Its purpose is to provide tools to understand, identify,
work through, and remove your limiting beliefs to achieve
growth and transformation. If you need additional support and
guidance, please seek the assistance of a professional coach or
therapist.

Printed in the United States of America
ISBN: 979-8-9873578-0-4

"For I know the plans I have for you," declares the Lord, "plans to prosper you and not to harm you, plans to give you hope and a future."

-Jeremiah 29:11

You have a story that is already written and waiting to be lived out. Believe in yourself so you can receive all of the blessings that are waiting for you.

~Harriet M. Harris, MBA

This Journal Belongs To:

_____

CONTENTS

PREFACE

Two years before I created this journal, I didn't know what a limiting belief was, let alone its impact on my life. And I certainly didn't know how to address or change them. I believed my life would always be hard, and I felt I had no control over that. I convinced myself that my life circumstances had brought me to where I was and that there was nothing I could do to change it.

I felt powerless.

I knew my life's path did not align with my true purpose. Even though I didn't feel I was on the right path, I kept pursuing success. All while constantly feeling as if I was living a life created for someone else.

I would often try one new thing after another, looking for that one thing that would elevate me to the level of success I desired in my life, but each time I tried something new, it didn't work as well as I had hoped. I thought something was wrong with me and that I didn't deserve nor would I ever achieve the life I desired.

In my mind, I was simply unlucky. I often said, "If something bad is going to happen, it'll happen to me." That's how I summed up my life.

Isn't that just sad?

I felt stuck and frustrated, as if I were a victim of events I had no control over. Even though I had nothing but good intentions for my life, it felt like I was repeatedly attracting negative situations over and over again.

I failed to see that something was missing from my life— something that held immense value but of which I had never been fully aware.

Belief in myself!

For years, I had been sabotaging my own success with my negative thoughts without even knowing it.

At some point in my life, I developed a belief that convinced me I wasn't good enough for exceptional things to happen because I'd allowed the bad experiences I'd had to overpower my ability to believe in myself and what I could achieve.

My bad experiences had created a belief in my mind that I was a magnet for bad things. Despite all the good things that had happened in my life, this belief was so strong that it kept me stuck in a cycle of always believing that something would go wrong.

Despite challenges and difficult life experiences, I have been fortunate in many ways. God has provided many blessings through good people, experiences, and opportunities. Unfortunately, I allowed my negative beliefs to block me from focusing on the positive things that also happened in my life.

My negative beliefs about myself were so deep-rooted in my mind that they prevented me from believing I deserved good things because of the bad experiences that I'd had.

I unknowingly allowed my bad experiences to restrict me from dreaming big, believing in myself, and believing that I deserved great things. I was dependent on the validation of others to feel good about myself, my ideas, and my achievements.

One day, while taking a long walk and in deep thought, I asked myself this question — "how can you expect anyone else to believe in you if you don't believe in yourself?"

I had become a prisoner of my own limiting beliefs and thought patterns—subconsciously writing the script for how my life would go and causing me not to reach my full potential in many areas of my life.

At that moment, I began a journey to discover myself, maybe for the first time in my adult life. This meant I had to confront some parts of my past that I had previously ignored or suppressed. It also meant that I had to learn to let go of old and unhealthy thoughts, beliefs, patterns, and habits holding me back from being the best version of myself.

It was time for me to discover myself and learn to believe in me.

I made a personal commitment to change how I thought about myself so that I could begin to see myself differently.

I began by reflecting on how I thought, spoke, and felt about myself. I also became more conscious of the thoughts and beliefs I had daily. It was shocking to to realize how much of what I thought, said, felt, and believed was negative. The more I reflected, the more aware I became of the self-limiting beliefs and thought patterns I had. I realized that my self-worth needed to come from within instead of looking for external validation from others. I started listening to my voice instead of letting other people's opinions control my life.

This process took a lot of time and even more patience. However, it was worth it because I learned to believe in myself, trust myself and value myself more than ever before. Maybe even for the very first time in my adult life.

I created this journal because I know that self-sabotage is real. I know that it is possible to be your own worst enemy and the biggest obstacle standing in the way of your success.

Our thoughts and beliefs can be the most powerful tools in our arsenal, but they can also be our biggest downfall.

This journal was designed to help <u>you</u> uncover <u>your</u> limiting beliefs and self-sabotaging thoughts so that you can: 1) create a vision for your life that aligns with who you desire to be and 2) begin to live from a place of authenticity. I hope and pray that the activities in this journal help you to discover what is holding you back from living the life of your dreams so that you can STOP STOPPING YOUR SUCCESS too!

My journey is ongoing, and success is part of my story. I know I am exactly where I need to be at this point in time, and my life is what it needs to be right now. Accepting this truth has allowed me to create a new vision of the life I want and the person I desire to be. I know that this journal's activities will help you do the same.

I hope you enjoy this journal as much as I enjoyed creating it.

Wishing you much success and happiness on your journey of self-discovery, healing, and growth!

Yours on the journey,

Harriet M. Harris, MBA

INTRODUCTION

It's time to take back your power and crush your limiting beliefs.

Limiting beliefs are the things you tell yourself that hold you back. They're the negative thoughts that keep you stuck and unable to reach your full potential. They're the voice in your head telling you that you can't do something or that someone else is better than you. They can be anything—from an idea drilled into your brain since childhood to a belief repeatedly reinforced by loved ones, friends, and even strangers.

BUT HERE'S THE THING:

Limiting beliefs aren't real. They're just thoughts! And we can change them if we want to.

In this journal, you'll be able to identify your limiting beliefs and then challenge them with the help of tools like journaling and writing prompts. This can help you to let go of your old, unhelpful beliefs and open yourself up to new ones that are better aligned with your goals. This journal aims to help you identify, understand, challenge, and change the limiting beliefs holding you back from success using the Six Rs to Ridding Limiting Beliefs process.

HOW TO USE THIS JOURNAL

This journal is a tool that you can use to help you recognize and release limiting beliefs. It is not meant to be done in one sitting but over time so as not to overload yourself with information. You did not acquire these beliefs overnight, so you will not be able to unlearn them overnight. It will take some time to unpack them.

The journal is divided into four parts. Start with Part 1 and complete each section consecutively to get the best results.

Part 1 will guide you through a journaling exercise that asks questions designed to help uncover how your current limiting beliefs are affecting your life and in what areas they may be holding you back—consciously or subconsciously. This exercise will help you discover the parts of your life where you may be stuck and how those feelings could affect your success.

Part 2 will help you identify the underlying limiting beliefs that are causing you to feel stuck in certain areas of your life. The questions in this section will help you uncover those beliefs so that you can begin working on changing them by reflecting on where the beliefs originated and challenging their validity.

Part 3 offers space for you to track and reflect on any new or recurring limiting beliefs, then use the Six Rs to Ridding Limiting Beliefs process to work through them. The quicker you are able to recognize and address a limiting belief, the less time it has to wreak havoc on your life.

Part 4 will help you assess your progress. This section will help you see how far you've come and allow you to celebrate your success.

Be aware that unlearning beliefs can be uncomfortable, but remember, we experience the most growth during periods of discomfort. You may experience negative emotions as you realize how much these beliefs have shaped your life and how they no longer serve you. You may grow frustrated with yourself or others around you who may have imposed some of the beliefs you uncover. Please give yourself (and others) grace as you navigate your way through unlearning those old, limiting thoughts and beliefs. These feelings and emotions are not uncommon to experience while unpacking negative beliefs. It's okay—it means you're doing it right!

Please take care of yourself as you go through this process. Refrain from forcing yourself through any of these steps if they make you too uncomfortable, and make sure that if it gets too overwhelming at any point, you stop for a while before continuing and come back later when you are ready to resume.

This journal will help you create healthy beliefs that allow you to live your best life! Your thoughts and beliefs have incredible power over your life. They can be incredibly positive, helping you reach your goals and create the life of your dreams. But they can also hold you back from living a full and happy life if they do not align with who you are, the life you want to live, or what is most important to you.

COMMIT TO EMBRACING CHANGE

While no one may see this contract that you are making with yourself, it is indeed still a contract —and it is a contract that you should take seriously. When you sign this contract with yourself, you promise to do whatever is necessary to reach your goals and commit to creating positive change in your life. But the most important thing about this contract is that you are being honest with yourself and making a promise to do whatever it takes to make those changes happen.

MY COMMITMENT TO ME

I _____ commit to embracing and making a change so that I can overcome my limiting beliefs and stop stopping my success.

I commit to continue seeking out new ways to improve myself, including challenging my own assumptions and evaluating my behaviors.

I commit to saying and doing things that make me feel empowered rather than disempowered.

I commit to embracing the way I feel and not fighting it.

I commit to sit with the discomfort of change and to allow myself to be uncomfortable.

I commit to taking action and making the necessary changes to live a fulfilling, happy, and exciting life.

I commit to using this journal as a tool for self-reflection and learning more about myself by writing down my thoughts each day (even if it's just a few sentences).

I commit myself fully to this journey of self-discovery and growth so that I may become better equipped with tools to help me overcome any obstacles or challenges that may come my way in life!

I want to be the best version of myself, and I know that I can't do that if I am unwilling to change my life. I will put in the work necessary to make this happen, and I will not give up until it does.

I will not wait for the perfect time, conditions, or person to come along. I will not wait for permission. I will take the first step towards creating change in my life today.

_____   _____
Signature   Date

WHAT IS A LIMITING BELIEF ANYWAY?

Limiting beliefs are thoughts that prevent us from moving toward our goals. They are negative beliefs about ourselves or the world around us. These limiting beliefs can make it hard for us to succeed because they create an invisible barrier between where we are now and where we want to be.

Believe it or not, every human has limiting beliefs. That's right, every one of us has things we believe about ourselves, the world, and others that keep us from living our best lives. For example, you may believe you aren't good enough or intelligent enough to do something. Or maybe you think you are a failure if you try something new and fail at it. You may also believe that other people are better than you or have more potential than you do. No matter what limiting belief has been holding you back —whether it's fear of failure, lack of confidence, low self-esteem, etc.—I'm here to tell you: It's time to release them!

Limiting beliefs are formed over time and often stem from childhood instilled into us by our parents, friends, or family. Other times these beliefs are the result of a traumatic experience. Sometimes there is no obvious explanation for where these beliefs originate. They are often subconscious and buried deep within our minds. But they still profoundly impact how we think, feel, and behave. In fact, your beliefs about yourself can be more limiting than any other factor in your life!

Limiting beliefs can be hard to recognize because they're irrational or untrue. For example: "I'm not good at math" - even if you're brilliant, everyone gets bad grades at some point. We don't always know why these thoughts get stuck inside our heads, but once they do, it's hard for them to go away on their own!

Here are just some of the most common limiting beliefs:

- I'm not good enough to achieve my goals.
- I can't do this.
- It's too hard or impossible.
- I'm not worthy.
- I'm not fit/thin/pretty enough.
- I'm not smart enough.
- I'm too old/young/tall/short to do this.
- I don't have enough money or time.
- I don't have enough experience.
- I'm not creative or smart enough to solve this problem.
- This is the way things are, and they will never change.

Limiting beliefs can trap you in a negative mindset that can be hard to escape. A negative mindset often leads to feelings of fear, anxiety, and self-doubt. These emotions can cause us to make poor decisions, often the opposite of what we want out of life. For example: If you have a limiting belief that "I am not good enough," this will affect your self-esteem and feelings about yourself. As a result, it could lead to fear or anxiety when facing challenges or difficult situations in life.

It is so important to understand and eliminate your limiting beliefs. By doing so, you can create a new mindset that supports you in living the life you want and allows you to move forward confidently.

In order to eliminate your limiting beliefs, it's essential to identify them first because you can't fix what you don't know is broken.

So let's get started!

GETTING RID OF LIMITING BELIEFS

The only way to stop allowing limiting beliefs to affect your success is to overcome them. To do this, you must discover what your limiting beliefs are and how they influence your thoughts or actions. The more you understand your limiting beliefs, the easier it will be for you to change them.

I wish I could tell you that there was an easy way to rid your mind of your limiting beliefs, but the truth is that it's a process. The only way to rid yourself of your limiting beliefs is by actively working through them. You can't just read an article or a blog and expect to be free of all your limiting beliefs. Instead, you must commit to learning about them and recognize when and how they affect your life. You have to be willing and ready to change and put in the work to overcome them. When you do this, you will notice how much easier it is to release the beliefs that have held you hostage, for so long. And if you stick with it, I promise it will be worth it!

Everyone is capable of changing their lives for the better by ridding their limiting beliefs. To do so, however, requires a process of self-reflection and transformation. The Six Rs to Ridding Limiting Beliefs is a process that will help you overcome limiting beliefs and create a life that you truly love if you willingly take the steps to — Recognize, Release, Reframe, Reclaim, Reshape and Receive.

1. Recognize your limiting beliefs

- The first step in overcoming a limiting belief is recognizing it exists, which can be difficult because they are often ingrained into your subconscious. You will need to clarify the negative thoughts, beliefs, and perceptions that have held you back. You can start by writing down your thoughts, feelings, and beliefs about a particular situation or experience.

2. Release the negative emotions that are associated with these beliefs

- You can release the negative emotions associated with a limiting belief by writing down all the feelings that come up when you think about it. This process can help you identify what's bothering you and makes you feel bad about yourself. Once you have determined how this belief impacts your emotional state and self-esteem, try to let go of the negative emotions by focusing on positive thoughts instead.

3. Reframe your thoughts

- This step is all about changing your mindset. You can reframe your thoughts by asking yourself questions such as: What is the opposite of what I believe (the limiting belief)? What evidence do I have that supports this belief? How does this belief impact my life and my goals? Instead of focusing on the negative belief, reframe it by focusing on how you would like that area of your life to be.

4. Reclaim control of your thoughts, beliefs, and life by taking action

- You are in the driver's seat of your life and have complete control of what does or does not happen. You have the power to create new beliefs, change your thoughts and actions, and take steps toward your goals. When you consciously decide to focus on positive thoughts, you will reclaim control over how you think and what you believe.

5. Reshape your reality by creating new empowering truths that support you and align with whom you want to be

- This step sits at the core of the process of overcoming limiting beliefs. Creating new empowering truths will allow you to free yourself from the false beliefs that have held you back and enable you to move forward with confidence and certainty. By reshaping your reality and creating new empowering truths, you will begin to view yourself more positively and be empowered to create the life you desire.

6. Receive all the good that comes your way by eliminating your limiting beliefs and embracing your new truths.

- Although each step is crucial for overcoming limiting beliefs, this step deserves special attention. When you eliminate your limiting beliefs and fully accept yourself, it becomes easier to let go of unnecessary suffering and feel worthy and deserving of all the good that will come your way.

This step is like opening a floodgate that allows positive energy to flow into your life, creating even more opportunities for prosperity, happiness, and success.

As new limiting beliefs emerge, you will have to REPEAT these steps until they become a part of your new reality.

Overcoming limiting beliefs will take time and patience. However, the benefits are more than worth the effort!

Part 1

START ASSESSING
YOUR THOUGHTS

IDENTIFY AREAS OF YOUR LIFE BEING AFFECTED BY YOUR BELIEFS

This journal section will challenge you to reflect on your life and how your limiting beliefs are holding you back from the life you desire. The questions in this section may make you uncomfortable, but that's a good thing—it means they're challenging your limiting beliefs!

Remember, being honest with yourself is crucial; this section will help you do that.

This section contains questions that will provide deeper insight into you and how you feel about your life. This is an integral part of the process because it allows you to gain more awareness. It also helps to put things into perspective so that you can move forward with more clarity on what needs to change in your life so you can live the life you desire.

Answering some of these questions might bring up sad memories or emotions. Acknowledge these feelings; they are a part of who you are and the journey you are about to take. Take comfort in knowing these feelings don't have to cause a permanent scar on your psyche. You are in control of your life and the only person capable of shifting your limiting beliefs.

ANSWER THE QUESTIONS BELOW TO DISCOVER HOW YOUR LIFE IS BEING AFFECTED BY LIMITING BELIEFS TODAY.

WHAT ARE SOME OF THE BIGGEST CHALLENGES YOU FACE IN YOUR LIFE THAT KEEP YOU FROM ACHIEVING THE THINGS THAT MATTER MOST TO YOU?

_____

_____

_____

_____

_____

_____

_____

_____

_____

OVERCOMING ONE OF THESE CHALLENGES WILL HAVE THE BIGGEST IMPACT ON YOUR LIFE. WHICH IS IT?

_____

_____

_____

_____

_____

_____

_____

_____

ON THE FOLLOWING PAGES, ANSWER THE QUESTIONS TO IDENTIFY AREAS WHERE YOU ARE BEING HELD BACK BY LIMITING BELIEFS.

ADDRESS ONE ITEM PER PAGE TO ENSURE THOROUGHNESS AND DETAILED THOUGHT FOR EACH AREA IDENTIFIED.

WHAT IS <u>ONE</u> AREA OF YOUR LIFE THAT YOU ARE UNSATISFIED WITH?

_____

_____

_____

_____

_____

_____

WHAT DO YOU DESIRE TO EXPERIENCE IN THIS AREA OF YOUR LIFE?

_____

_____

_____

_____

_____

_____

_____

WHAT KEEPS YOU FROM EXPERIENCING WHAT YOU DESIRE IN THIS AREA OF YOUR LIFE?

_____

_____

_____

_____

_____

_____

_____

WHAT IS <u>ONE</u> AREA OF YOUR LIFE THAT YOU ARE
UNSATISFIED WITH?

_____

_____

_____

_____

_____

_____

WHAT DO YOU DESIRE TO EXPERIENCE IN THIS AREA OF
YOUR LIFE?

_____

_____

_____

_____

_____

_____

WHAT KEEPS YOU FROM EXPERIENCING WHAT YOU DESIRE IN
THIS AREA OF YOUR LIFE?

_____

_____

_____

_____

_____

_____

WHAT IS <u>ONE</u> AREA OF YOUR LIFE THAT YOU ARE
UNSATISFIED WITH?

_____

_____

_____

_____

_____

_____

WHAT DO YOU DESIRE TO EXPERIENCE IN THIS AREA OF
YOUR LIFE?

_____

_____

_____

_____

_____

_____

WHAT KEEPS YOU FROM EXPERIENCING WHAT YOU DESIRE IN
THIS AREA OF YOUR LIFE?

_____

_____

_____

_____

_____

_____

WHAT IS <u>ONE</u> AREA OF YOUR LIFE THAT YOU ARE UNSATISFIED WITH?

_____

_____

_____

_____

_____

_____

WHAT DO YOU DESIRE TO EXPERIENCE IN THIS AREA OF YOUR LIFE?

_____

_____

_____

_____

_____

_____

WHAT KEEPS YOU FROM EXPERIENCING WHAT YOU DESIRE IN THIS AREA OF YOUR LIFE?

_____

_____

_____

_____

_____

_____

WHAT IS <u>ONE</u> AREA OF YOUR LIFE THAT YOU ARE
 UNSATISFIED WITH?

_____

_____

_____

_____

_____

_____

_____

WHAT DO YOU DESIRE TO EXPERIENCE IN THIS AREA OF
YOUR LIFE?

_____

_____

_____

_____

_____

_____

_____

WHAT KEEPS YOU FROM EXPERIENCING WHAT YOU DESIRE IN
THIS AREA OF YOUR LIFE?

_____

_____

_____

_____

_____

_____

_____

WHAT IS <u>ONE</u> AREA OF YOUR LIFE THAT YOU ARE
 UNSATISFIED WITH?

_____

_____

_____

_____

_____

_____

WHAT DO YOU DESIRE TO EXPERIENCE IN THIS AREA OF
YOUR LIFE?

_____

_____

_____

_____

_____

_____

WHAT KEEPS YOU FROM EXPERIENCING WHAT YOU DESIRE IN
THIS AREA OF YOUR LIFE?

_____

_____

_____

_____

_____

_____

WHAT IS <u>ONE</u> AREA OF YOUR LIFE THAT YOU ARE
 UNSATISFIED WITH?

_____

_____

_____

_____

_____

_____

_____

WHAT DO YOU DESIRE TO EXPERIENCE IN THIS AREA OF
YOUR LIFE?

_____

_____

_____

_____

_____

_____

_____

WHAT KEEPS YOU FROM EXPERIENCING WHAT YOU DESIRE IN
THIS AREA OF YOUR LIFE?

_____

_____

_____

_____

_____

_____

_____

WHAT IS <u>ONE</u> AREA OF YOUR LIFE THAT YOU ARE
UNSATISFIED WITH?

_____

_____

_____

_____

_____

_____

WHAT DO YOU DESIRE TO EXPERIENCE IN THIS AREA OF
YOUR LIFE?

_____

_____

_____

_____

_____

_____

WHAT KEEPS YOU FROM EXPERIENCING WHAT YOU DESIRE IN
THIS AREA OF YOUR LIFE?

_____

_____

_____

_____

_____

_____

WHAT IS <u>ONE</u> AREA OF YOUR LIFE THAT YOU ARE
  UNSATISFIED WITH?

_____

_____

_____

_____

_____

_____

_____

WHAT DO YOU DESIRE TO EXPERIENCE IN THIS AREA OF
YOUR LIFE?

_____

_____

_____

_____

_____

_____

_____

WHAT KEEPS YOU FROM EXPERIENCING WHAT YOU DESIRE IN
THIS AREA OF YOUR LIFE?

_____

_____

_____

_____

_____

_____

_____

WHAT IS <u>ONE</u> AREA OF YOUR LIFE THAT YOU ARE
UNSATISFIED WITH?

_____

_____

_____

_____

_____

_____

WHAT DO YOU DESIRE TO EXPERIENCE IN THIS AREA OF
YOUR LIFE?

_____

_____

_____

_____

_____

_____

WHAT KEEPS YOU FROM EXPERIENCING WHAT YOU DESIRE IN
THIS AREA OF YOUR LIFE?

_____

_____

_____

_____

_____

_____

THE POWER OF "I CAN'T"

It can be easy to identify our own personal limitations. Limiting beliefs often begin with the words "I can't." We often say things like, "I can't do this" or "I'm not good at that." These beliefs are limiting because they tell us that we're incapable of doing certain things. They can also be very damaging because they make us feel inferior and less worthy.

Think about the things you often say you can't do to begin identifying your limiting beliefs. Are there any recurring patterns? How often do you say these things to yourself? Is it more than once a day? If so, these beliefs may be holding you back from reaching your full potential.

Let's start by identifying your "I can't" beliefs.

ON THE PAGES THAT FOLLOW, ANSWER THE QUESTIONS TO IDENTIFY WHERE YOU ARE FEELING STUCK AND WHY.

ADDRESS ONE AREA PER PAGE TO GET THE MOST FROM THIS EXERCISE. CONSIDER ALL ASPECTS OF YOUR LIFE—SOCIAL, FINANCIAL, PERSONAL RELATIONSHIPS, CAREER, HEALTH AND WELLNESS, EDUCATION/SCHOOLING.

WHAT IS <u>ONE</u> AREA OF YOUR LIFE THAT YOU FEEL STUCK?

_____

_____

_____

_____

_____

_____

WHY DO YOU FEEL STUCK IN THIS AREA?

_____

_____

_____

_____

_____

_____

_____

CREATE A SENTENCE BASED ON YOUR RESPONSES ABOVE

EX. I CAN'T <u>START A BUSINESS</u> (WHAT) BECAUSE <u>I AM NOT CREATIVE ENOUGH</u> (WHY).

I CAN'T _____

BECAUSE _____

_____ .

WHAT REASON ARE YOU USING AS AN EXCUSE FOR NOT TAKING ACTION TO ACHIEVE THIS?

LIST THE REASON AFTER THE WORD "BECAUSE" ON THE PREVIOUS PAGE.
EX. <u>I AM NOT CREATIVE ENOUGH.</u>

_____

_____

_____

_____

_____

_____

WHERE DO YOU THINK THIS BELIEF CAME FROM?

_____

_____

_____

_____

_____

_____

HAVE YOU PROVEN THIS BELIEF TO BE TRUE?

_____

_____

_____

_____

_____

_____

WHAT IS <u>ONE</u> AREA OF YOUR LIFE THAT YOU FEEL STUCK?

_____

_____

_____

_____

_____

_____

WHY DO YOU FEEL STUCK IN THIS AREA?

_____

_____

_____

_____

_____

_____

CREATE A SENTENCE BASED ON YOUR RESPONSES ABOVE

EX. I CAN'T <u>START A BUSINESS</u> (WHAT) BECAUSE <u>I AM NOT CREATIVE ENOUGH</u> (WHY).

I CAN'T _____

BECAUSE _____

_____.

WHAT REASON ARE YOU USING AS AN EXCUSE FOR NOT TAKING ACTION TO ACHIEVE THIS?

LIST THE REASON AFTER THE WORD "BECAUSE" ON THE PREVIOUS PAGE.
EX. <u>I AM NOT CREATIVE ENOUGH.</u>

_____

_____

_____

_____

_____

WHERE DO YOU THINK THIS BELIEF CAME FROM?

_____

_____

_____

_____

_____

HAVE YOU PROVEN THIS BELIEF TO BE TRUE?

_____

_____

_____

_____

_____

_____

WHAT IS <u>ONE</u> AREA OF YOUR LIFE THAT YOU FEEL STUCK?

_____

_____

_____

_____

_____

_____

WHY DO YOU FEEL STUCK IN THIS AREA?

_____

_____

_____

_____

_____

_____

CREATE A SENTENCE BASED ON YOUR RESPONSES ABOVE

EX. I CAN'T <u>START A BUSINESS</u> (WHAT) BECAUSE <u>I AM NOT CREATIVE ENOUGH</u> (WHY).

I CAN'T _____

BECAUSE _____

_____ .

WHAT REASON ARE YOU USING AS AN EXCUSE FOR NOT TAKING ACTION TO ACHIEVE THIS?

LIST THE REASON AFTER THE WORD "BECAUSE" ON THE PREVIOUS PAGE.
EX. I AM NOT CREATIVE ENOUGH.

_____

_____

_____

_____

_____

_____

WHERE DO YOU THINK THIS BELIEF CAME FROM?

_____

_____

_____

_____

_____

_____

HAVE YOU PROVEN THIS BELIEF TO BE TRUE?

_____

_____

_____

_____

_____

_____

WHAT IS <u>ONE</u> AREA OF YOUR LIFE THAT YOU FEEL STUCK?

_____

_____

_____

_____

_____

_____

WHY DO YOU FEEL STUCK IN THIS AREA?

_____

_____

_____

_____

_____

_____

CREATE A SENTENCE BASED ON YOUR RESPONSES ABOVE

EX. I CAN'T <u>START A BUSINESS</u> (WHAT) BECAUSE <u>I AM NOT CREATIVE ENOUGH</u> (WHY).

I CAN'T _____

BECAUSE _____

_____.

WHAT REASON ARE YOU USING AS AN EXCUSE FOR NOT TAKING ACTION TO ACHIEVE THIS?

LIST THE REASON AFTER THE WORD "BECAUSE" ON THE PREVIOUS PAGE.
EX. I AM NOT CREATIVE ENOUGH.

_____

_____

_____

_____

_____

_____

WHERE DO YOU THINK THIS BELIEF CAME FROM?

_____

_____

_____

_____

_____

_____

HAVE YOU PROVEN THIS BELIEF TO BE TRUE?

_____

_____

_____

_____

_____

_____

WHAT IS <u>ONE</u> AREA OF YOUR LIFE THAT YOU FEEL STUCK?

_____

_____

_____

_____

_____

_____

_____

WHY DO YOU FEEL STUCK IN THIS AREA?

_____

_____

_____

_____

_____

_____

_____

CREATE A SENTENCE BASED ON YOUR RESPONSES ABOVE

EX. I CAN'T <u>START A BUSINESS</u> (WHAT) BECAUSE <u>I AM NOT CREATIVE ENOUGH</u> (WHY).

I CAN'T _____

BECAUSE _____

_____ .

WHAT REASON ARE YOU USING AS AN EXCUSE FOR NOT TAKING ACTION TO ACHIEVE THIS?

LIST THE REASON AFTER THE WORD "BECAUSE" ON THE PREVIOUS PAGE.
EX. <u>I AM NOT CREATIVE ENOUGH.</u>

_____

_____

_____

_____

_____

_____

WHERE DO YOU THINK THIS BELIEF CAME FROM?

_____

_____

_____

_____

_____

_____

HAVE YOU PROVEN THIS BELIEF TO BE TRUE?

_____

_____

_____

_____

_____

_____

WHAT IS <u>ONE</u> AREA OF YOUR LIFE THAT YOU FEEL STUCK?

_____

_____

_____

_____

_____

_____

_____

WHY DO YOU FEEL STUCK IN THIS AREA?

_____

_____

_____

_____

_____

_____

_____

CREATE A SENTENCE BASED ON YOUR RESPONSES ABOVE

EX. I CAN'T <u>START A BUSINESS</u> (WHAT) BECAUSE <u>I AM NOT CREATIVE ENOUGH</u> (WHY).

I CAN'T _____

BECAUSE _____

_____.

WHAT REASON ARE YOU USING AS AN EXCUSE FOR NOT TAKING ACTION TO ACHIEVE THIS?

LIST THE REASON AFTER THE WORD "BECAUSE" ON THE PREVIOUS PAGE.
EX. I AM NOT CREATIVE ENOUGH.

_____
_____
_____
_____
_____
_____

WHERE DO YOU THINK THIS BELIEF CAME FROM?

_____
_____
_____
_____
_____
_____

HAVE YOU PROVEN THIS BELIEF TO BE TRUE?

_____
_____
_____
_____
_____
_____

WHAT IS <u>ONE</u> AREA OF YOUR LIFE THAT YOU FEEL STUCK?

_____

_____

_____

_____

_____

_____

WHY DO YOU FEEL STUCK IN THIS AREA?

_____

_____

_____

_____

_____

_____

CREATE A SENTENCE BASED ON YOUR RESPONSES ABOVE

EX. I CAN'T <u>START A BUSINESS</u> (WHAT) BECAUSE <u>I AM NOT CREATIVE ENOUGH</u> (WHY).

I CAN'T _____

BECAUSE _____

_____.

WHAT REASON ARE YOU USING AS AN EXCUSE FOR NOT TAKING ACTION TO ACHIEVE THIS?

LIST THE REASON AFTER THE WORD "BECAUSE" ON THE PREVIOUS PAGE.
EX. <u>I AM NOT CREATIVE ENOUGH.</u>

_____

_____

_____

_____

_____

_____

WHERE DO YOU THINK THIS BELIEF CAME FROM?

_____

_____

_____

_____

_____

_____

HAVE YOU PROVEN THIS BELIEF TO BE TRUE?

_____

_____

_____

_____

_____

_____

WHAT IS <u>ONE</u> AREA OF YOUR LIFE THAT YOU FEEL STUCK?

_____

_____

_____

_____

_____

_____

_____

WHY DO YOU FEEL STUCK IN THIS AREA?

_____

_____

_____

_____

_____

_____

_____

CREATE A SENTENCE BASED ON YOUR RESPONSES ABOVE

EX. I CAN'T <u>START A BUSINESS</u> (WHAT) BECAUSE <u>I AM NOT CREATIVE ENOUGH </u>(WHY).

I CAN'T _____

BECAUSE _____

_____ .

WHAT REASON ARE YOU USING AS AN EXCUSE FOR NOT TAKING ACTION TO ACHIEVE THIS?

LIST THE REASON AFTER THE WORD "BECAUSE" ON THE PREVIOUS PAGE.
EX. <u>I AM NOT CREATIVE ENOUGH.</u>

_____

_____

_____

_____

_____

WHERE DO YOU THINK THIS BELIEF CAME FROM?

_____

_____

_____

_____

_____

HAVE YOU PROVEN THIS BELIEF TO BE TRUE?

_____

_____

_____

_____

_____

WHAT IS <u>ONE</u> AREA OF YOUR LIFE THAT YOU FEEL STUCK?

_____

_____

_____

_____

_____

_____

WHY DO YOU FEEL STUCK IN THIS AREA?

_____

_____

_____

_____

_____

_____

CREATE A SENTENCE BASED ON YOUR RESPONSES ABOVE

EX. I CAN'T <u>START A BUSINESS</u> (WHAT) BECAUSE <u>I AM NOT CREATIVE ENOUGH</u> (WHY).

I CAN'T _____

BECAUSE _____

_____.

WHAT REASON ARE YOU USING AS AN EXCUSE FOR NOT TAKING ACTION TO ACHIEVE THIS?

LIST THE REASON AFTER THE WORD "BECAUSE' ON THE PREVIOUS PAGE.
EX. <u>I AM NOT CREATIVE ENOUGH.</u>

_____

_____

_____

_____

_____

_____

WHERE DO YOU THINK THIS BELIEF CAME FROM?

_____

_____

_____

_____

_____

_____

HAVE YOU PROVEN THIS BELIEF TO BE TRUE?

_____

_____

_____

_____

_____

_____

WHAT IS <u>ONE</u> AREA OF YOUR LIFE THAT YOU FEEL STUCK?

_____

_____

_____

_____

_____

_____

_____

WHY DO YOU FEEL STUCK IN THIS AREA?

_____

_____

_____

_____

_____

_____

_____

CREATE A SENTENCE BASED ON YOUR RESPONSES ABOVE

EX. I CAN'T <u>START A BUSINESS</u> (WHAT) BECAUSE <u>I AM NOT CREATIVE ENOUGH</u> (WHY).

I CAN'T _____

BECAUSE _____

_____.

WHAT REASON ARE YOU USING AS AN EXCUSE FOR NOT TAKING ACTION TO ACHIEVE THIS?

LIST THE REASON AFTER THE WORD "BECAUSE" ON THE PREVIOUS PAGE.
EX. <u>I AM NOT CREATIVE ENOUGH.</u>

_____

_____

_____

_____

_____

_____

WHERE DO YOU THINK THIS BELIEF CAME FROM?

_____

_____

_____

_____

_____

_____

HAVE YOU PROVEN THIS BELIEF TO BE TRUE?

_____

_____

_____

_____

_____

_____

WHAT IS <u>ONE</u> AREA OF YOUR LIFE THAT YOU FEEL STUCK?

_____

_____

_____

_____

_____

_____

_____

WHY DO YOU FEEL STUCK IN THIS AREA?

_____

_____

_____

_____

_____

_____

_____

CREATE A SENTENCE BASED ON YOUR RESPONSES ABOVE

EX. I CAN'T <u>START A BUSINESS</u> (WHAT) BECAUSE <u>I AM NOT CREATIVE ENOUGH </u>(WHY).

I CAN'T _____

BECAUSE _____

_____.

WHAT REASON ARE YOU USING AS AN EXCUSE FOR NOT TAKING ACTION TO ACHIEVE THIS?

LIST THE REASON AFTER THE WORD "BECAUSE" ON THE PREVIOUS PAGE.
EX. <u>I AM NOT CREATIVE ENOUGH.</u>

_____

_____

_____

_____

_____

_____

WHERE DO YOU THINK THIS BELIEF CAME FROM?

_____

_____

_____

_____

_____

_____

HAVE YOU PROVEN THIS BELIEF TO BE TRUE?

_____

_____

_____

_____

_____

_____

Part 2

START REWRITING
YOUR SCRIPT

IDENTIFY YOUR CURRENT LIMITING BELIEFS

In this section, you will confront and work through the limiting beliefs that have inhibited your success. You will use the steps in the Six Rs to Ridding Limiting Beliefs process to: recognize the thoughts and emotions that have been holding you back, release them, reframe your mindset, reclaim your power, reshape your reality and be ready to receive all the good coming your way.

As you begin to think about your limiting beliefs, consider the following questions for each limiting belief you identify:

- Where did this belief come from?
- Is it something that was said to or about you?
- Why do you believe this?
- Have you proven these beliefs to be true?

As you write out each belief and challenge it, ask yourself in what ways you see this belief to be true. When we have a belief that limits us, it often shows up in our lives in patterns or behaviors that keep us stuck.

For example, let's say you believe you are not good enough, and because of this belief, you don't ask for promotions at work or even consider opportunities that would benefit your career. You may never get the promotion if you don't go after it, but that doesn't mean you are not good enough. It simply means you didn't try. This belief limits your life and keeps you stuck in place.

You may also feel you are "not good enough" in your personal life and, as a result, not pursue relationships, friendships, or activities that would bring you more joy. As you challenge your limiting beliefs, you can start to see how these beliefs are holding you back in different areas of your life.

If you are still determining whether some of your beliefs might be limiting you, review the list of common limiting beliefs below to determine if any fit you personally as you begin your exploration.

Common Limiting Beliefs:
- I'm not good with money.
- I don't have enough time to invest in myself.
- I can't earn a six-figure income because I don't have the talent or knowledge to do so.
- I don't have enough time.
- I can't start a business because it is too expensive.
- I can't get good grades because I'm just not smart.
- I can't go back to college because I'm too old.
- I'm not good enough.
- Not trying is better than failing.
- I don't deserve nice things.
- No one will care what I have to say.
- I can't be my authentic self, or I'll be judged.
- I can't ask for what I want because I may get rejected.

In this section, you will list your limiting beliefs and work through each one to uncover the truth behind them.

LIST A BELIEF YOU HAVE ABOUT YOURSELF THAT KEEPS YOU
FROM BEING THE VERSION OF YOURSELF THAT YOU DESIRE
TO BE.

_____

_____

_____

_____

_____

_____

_____

IS THIS BELIEF TRUE? WHY OR WHY NOT?

_____

_____

_____

_____

WHERE DOES THIS BELIEF COME FROM?
EVALUATE THE SOURCES TO HELP DETERMINE IF THEY HAVE ANY VALIDITY IN
YOUR LIFE TODAY.

_____

_____

_____

_____

_____

_____

HOW HAS THIS BELIEF AFFECTED YOUR LIFE UP UNTIL NOW? WHAT HAS THIS BELIEF PREVENTED YOU FROM DOING?

_____

_____

_____

_____

_____

_____

_____

_____

_____

_____

_____

_____

_____

_____

_____

_____

_____

_____

_____

_____

HOW WOULD YOUR LIFE CHANGE IF YOU ELIMINATED THIS
BELIEF?

_____

_____

_____

_____

_____

_____

WHAT POSITIVE BELIEFS WOULD BE BETTER FOR HELPING
YOU ATTAIN YOUR GOALS? CREATE A NEW EMPOWERING
TRUTH USING THESE POSITIVE BELIEFS.

_____

_____

_____

_____

_____

WHAT EVIDENCE SUPPORTS THIS NEW TRUTH? HOW DOES
THIS NEW TRUTH MAKE YOU FEEL?

_____

_____

_____

_____

_____

_____

IF YOU ADOPTED THIS NEW BELIEF AND APPLIED IT TO YOUR LIFE, WHAT WOULD BE DIFFERENT IN YOUR LIFE?

_____

_____

_____

_____

_____

_____

_____

_____

_____

_____

_____

_____

_____

_____

_____

_____

_____

_____

_____

_____

_____

_____

_____

_____

LIST A BELIEF YOU HAVE ABOUT YOURSELF THAT KEEPS YOU
FROM BEING THE VERSION OF YOURSELF THAT YOU DESIRE
TO BE.

_____

_____

_____

_____

_____

_____

_____

IS THIS BELIEF TRUE? WHY OR WHY NOT?

_____

_____

_____

_____

WHERE DOES THIS BELIEF COME FROM?
EVALUATE THE SOURCES TO HELP DETERMINE IF THEY HAVE ANY VALIDITY IN
YOUR LIFE TODAY.

_____

_____

_____

_____

_____

_____

HOW HAS THIS BELIEF AFFECTED YOUR LIFE UP UNTIL NOW? WHAT HAS THIS BELIEF PREVENTED YOU FROM DOING?

_____

_____

_____

_____

_____

_____

_____

_____

_____

_____

_____

_____

_____

_____

_____

_____

_____

_____

_____

_____

_____

_____

HOW WOULD YOUR LIFE CHANGE IF YOU ELIMINATED THIS BELIEF?

_____

_____

_____

_____

_____

_____

WHAT POSITIVE BELIEFS WOULD BE BETTER FOR HELPING YOU ATTAIN YOUR GOALS? CREATE A NEW EMPOWERING TRUTH USING THESE POSITIVE BELIEFS.

_____

_____

_____

_____

_____

WHAT EVIDENCE SUPPORTS THIS NEW TRUTH? HOW DOES THIS NEW TRUTH MAKE YOU FEEL?

_____

_____

_____

_____

_____

_____

IF YOU ADOPTED THIS NEW BELIEF AND APPLIED IT TO YOUR LIFE, WHAT WOULD BE DIFFERENT IN YOUR LIFE?

_____

_____

_____

_____

_____

_____

_____

_____

_____

_____

_____

_____

_____

_____

_____

_____

_____

_____

_____

_____

LIST A BELIEF YOU HAVE ABOUT YOURSELF THAT KEEPS YOU
FROM BEING THE VERSION OF YOURSELF THAT YOU DESIRE
TO BE.

_____

_____

_____

_____

_____

_____

_____

IS THIS BELIEF TRUE? WHY OR WHY NOT?

_____

_____

_____

_____

WHERE DOES THIS BELIEF COME FROM?
EVALUATE THE SOURCES TO HELP DETERMINE IF THEY HAVE ANY VALIDITY IN
YOUR LIFE TODAY.

_____

_____

_____

_____

_____

_____

HOW HAS THIS BELIEF AFFECTED YOUR LIFE UP UNTIL NOW? WHAT HAS THIS BELIEF PREVENTED YOU FROM DOING?

HOW WOULD YOUR LIFE CHANGE IF YOU ELIMINATED THIS BELIEF?

_____

_____

_____

_____

_____

_____

_____

WHAT POSITIVE BELIEFS WOULD BE BETTER FOR HELPING YOU ATTAIN YOUR GOALS? CREATE A NEW EMPOWERING TRUTH USING THESE POSITIVE BELIEFS.

_____

_____

_____

_____

_____

_____

WHAT EVIDENCE SUPPORTS THIS NEW TRUTH? HOW DOES THIS NEW TRUTH MAKE YOU FEEL?

_____

_____

_____

_____

_____

_____

_____

IF YOU ADOPTED THIS NEW BELIEF AND APPLIED IT TO YOUR LIFE, WHAT WOULD BE DIFFERENT IN YOUR LIFE?

LIST A BELIEF THAT YOU ARE HOLDING ONTO THAT IS
KEEPING YOU FROM BEING THE VERSION OF YOU THAT YOU
TRULY DESIRE TO BE.

_____

_____

_____

_____

_____

_____

_____

IS THIS BELIEF TRUE? WHY OR WHY NOT?

_____

_____

_____

_____

_____

WHERE DOES THIS BELIEF COME FROM?
EVALUATE THE SOURCES TO HELP DETERMINE IF THEY HAVE ANY VALIDITY IN
YOUR LIFE TODAY.

_____

_____

_____

_____

_____

_____

HOW HAS THIS BELIEF AFFECTED YOUR LIFE UP UNTIL NOW? WHAT HAS THIS BELIEF PREVENTED YOU FROM DOING?

HOW WOULD YOUR LIFE CHANGE IF YOU ELIMINATED THIS BELIEF?

_____

_____

_____

_____

_____

_____

_____

WHAT POSITIVE BELIEFS WOULD BE BETTER FOR HELPING YOU ATTAIN YOUR GOALS? CREATE A NEW EMPOWERING TRUTH USING THESE POSITIVE BELIEFS.

_____

_____

_____

_____

_____

_____

WHAT EVIDENCE SUPPORTS THIS NEW TRUTH? HOW DOES THIS NEW TRUTH MAKE YOU FEEL?

_____

_____

_____

_____

_____

_____

_____

IF YOU ADOPTED THIS NEW BELIEF AND APPLIED IT TO YOUR
LIFE, WHAT WOULD BE DIFFERENT IN YOUR LIFE?

LIST A BELIEF YOU HAVE ABOUT YOURSELF THAT KEEPS YOU
FROM BEING THE VERSION OF YOURSELF THAT YOU DESIRE
TO BE.

_____

_____

_____

_____

_____

_____

_____

_____

IS THIS BELIEF TRUE? WHY OR WHY NOT?

_____

_____

_____

_____

_____

WHERE DOES THIS BELIEF COME FROM?
EVALUATE THE SOURCES TO HELP DETERMINE IF THEY HAVE ANY VALIDITY IN
YOUR LIFE TODAY.

_____

_____

_____

_____

_____

_____

HOW HAS THIS BELIEF AFFECTED YOUR LIFE UP UNTIL NOW? WHAT HAS THIS BELIEF PREVENTED YOU FROM DOING?

HOW WOULD YOUR LIFE CHANGE IF YOU ELIMINATED THIS BELIEF?

_____

_____

_____

_____

_____

_____

WHAT POSITIVE BELIEFS WOULD BE BETTER FOR HELPING YOU ATTAIN YOUR GOALS? CREATE A NEW EMPOWERING TRUTH USING THESE POSITIVE BELIEFS.

_____

_____

_____

_____

_____

_____

WHAT EVIDENCE SUPPORTS THIS NEW TRUTH? HOW DOES THIS NEW TRUTH MAKE YOU FEEL?

_____

_____

_____

_____

_____

_____

IF YOU ADOPTED THIS NEW BELIEF AND APPLIED IT TO YOUR
LIFE, WHAT WOULD BE DIFFERENT IN YOUR LIFE?

LIST A BELIEF YOU HAVE ABOUT YOURSELF THAT KEEPS YOU
FROM BEING THE VERSION OF YOURSELF THAT YOU DESIRE
TO BE.

_____

_____

_____

_____

_____

_____

IS THIS BELIEF TRUE? WHY OR WHY NOT?

_____

_____

_____

_____

WHERE DOES THIS BELIEF COME FROM?
EVALUATE THE SOURCES TO HELP DETERMINE IF THEY HAVE ANY VALIDITY IN
YOUR LIFE TODAY.

_____

_____

_____

_____

_____

_____

HOW HAS THIS BELIEF AFFECTED YOUR LIFE UP UNTIL NOW? WHAT HAS THIS BELIEF PREVENTED YOU FROM DOING?

HOW WOULD YOUR LIFE CHANGE IF YOU ELIMINATED THIS BELIEF?

_____

_____

_____

_____

_____

_____

WHAT POSITIVE BELIEFS WOULD BE BETTER FOR HELPING YOU ATTAIN YOUR GOALS? CREATE A NEW EMPOWERING TRUTH USING THESE POSITIVE BELIEFS.

_____

_____

_____

_____

_____

WHAT EVIDENCE SUPPORTS THIS NEW TRUTH? HOW DOES THIS NEW TRUTH MAKE YOU FEEL?

_____

_____

_____

_____

_____

_____

IF YOU ADOPTED THIS NEW BELIEF AND APPLIED IT TO YOUR
LIFE, WHAT WOULD BE DIFFERENT IN YOUR LIFE?

_____

_____

_____

_____

_____

_____

_____

_____

_____

_____

_____

_____

_____

_____

_____

_____

_____

_____

_____

_____

_____

_____

_____

_____

LIST A BELIEF YOU HAVE ABOUT YOURSELF THAT KEEPS YOU
FROM BEING THE VERSION OF YOURSELF THAT YOU DESIRE
TO BE.

_____

_____

_____

_____

_____

_____

_____

_____

IS THIS BELIEF TRUE? WHY OR WHY NOT?

_____

_____

_____

_____

_____

WHERE DOES THIS BELIEF COME FROM?
EVALUATE THE SOURCES TO HELP DETERMINE IF THEY HAVE ANY VALIDITY IN
YOUR LIFE TODAY.

_____

_____

_____

_____

_____

_____

HOW HAS THIS BELIEF AFFECTED YOUR LIFE UP UNTIL NOW? WHAT HAS THIS BELIEF PREVENTED YOU FROM DOING?

HOW WOULD YOUR LIFE CHANGE IF YOU ELIMINATED THIS BELIEF?

_____

_____

_____

_____

_____

_____

WHAT POSITIVE BELIEFS WOULD BE BETTER FOR HELPING YOU ATTAIN YOUR GOALS? CREATE A NEW EMPOWERING TRUTH USING THESE POSITIVE BELIEFS.

_____

_____

_____

_____

_____

_____

WHAT EVIDENCE SUPPORTS THIS NEW TRUTH? HOW DOES THIS NEW TRUTH MAKE YOU FEEL?

_____

_____

_____

_____

_____

_____

IF YOU ADOPTED THIS NEW BELIEF AND APPLIED IT TO YOUR
LIFE, WHAT WOULD BE DIFFERENT IN YOUR LIFE?

LIST A BELIEF YOU HAVE ABOUT YOURSELF THAT KEEPS YOU
FROM BEING THE VERSION OF YOURSELF THAT YOU DESIRE
TO BE.

_____

_____

_____

_____

_____

_____

_____

IS THIS BELIEF TRUE? WHY OR WHY NOT?

_____

_____

_____

_____

WHERE DOES THIS BELIEF COME FROM?
EVALUATE THE SOURCES TO HELP DETERMINE IF THEY HAVE ANY VALIDITY IN
YOUR LIFE TODAY.

_____

_____

_____

_____

_____

HOW HAS THIS BELIEF AFFECTED YOUR LIFE UP UNTIL NOW? WHAT HAS THIS BELIEF PREVENTED YOU FROM DOING?

_____

_____

_____

_____

_____

_____

_____

_____

_____

_____

_____

_____

_____

_____

_____

_____

_____

_____

_____

_____

_____

_____

_____

_____

_____

_____

HOW WOULD YOUR LIFE CHANGE IF YOU ELIMINATED THIS
BELIEF?

_____

_____

_____

_____

_____

_____

_____

WHAT POSITIVE BELIEFS WOULD BE BETTER FOR HELPING
YOU ATTAIN YOUR GOALS? CREATE A NEW EMPOWERING
TRUTH USING THESE POSITIVE BELIEFS.

_____

_____

_____

_____

_____

_____

WHAT EVIDENCE SUPPORTS THIS NEW TRUTH? HOW DOES
THIS NEW TRUTH MAKE YOU FEEL?

_____

_____

_____

_____

_____

_____

IF YOU ADOPTED THIS NEW BELIEF AND APPLIED IT TO YOUR
LIFE, WHAT WOULD BE DIFFERENT IN YOUR LIFE?

LIST A BELIEF YOU HAVE ABOUT YOURSELF THAT KEEPS YOU
FROM BEING THE VERSION OF YOURSELF THAT YOU DESIRE
TO BE.

_____

_____

_____

_____

_____

_____

_____

_____

IS THIS BELIEF TRUE? WHY OR WHY NOT?

_____

_____

_____

_____

_____

WHERE DOES THIS BELIEF COME FROM?
EVALUATE THE SOURCES TO HELP DETERMINE IF THEY HAVE ANY VALIDITY IN
YOUR LIFE TODAY.

_____

_____

_____

_____

_____

_____

HOW HAS THIS BELIEF AFFECTED YOUR LIFE UP UNTIL NOW? WHAT HAS THIS BELIEF PREVENTED YOU FROM DOING?

_____

_____

_____

_____

_____

_____

_____

_____

_____

_____

_____

_____

_____

_____

_____

_____

_____

_____

_____

_____

_____

_____

_____

_____

HOW WOULD YOUR LIFE CHANGE IF YOU ELIMINATED THIS BELIEF?

_____

_____

_____

_____

_____

_____

WHAT POSITIVE BELIEFS WOULD BE BETTER FOR HELPING YOU ATTAIN YOUR GOALS? CREATE A NEW EMPOWERING TRUTH USING THESE POSITIVE BELIEFS.

_____

_____

_____

_____

_____

WHAT EVIDENCE SUPPORTS THIS NEW TRUTH? HOW DOES THIS NEW TRUTH MAKE YOU FEEL?

_____

_____

_____

_____

_____

_____

IF YOU ADOPTED THIS NEW BELIEF AND APPLIED IT TO YOUR
LIFE, WHAT WOULD BE DIFFERENT IN YOUR LIFE?

_____

_____

_____

_____

_____

_____

_____

_____

_____

_____

_____

_____

_____

_____

_____

_____

_____

_____

_____

_____

_____

_____

_____

_____

_____

_____

LIST A BELIEF YOU HAVE ABOUT YOURSELF THAT KEEPS YOU
FROM BEING THE VERSION OF YOURSELF THAT YOU DESIRE
TO BE.

_____

_____

_____

_____

_____

_____

_____

IS THIS BELIEF TRUE? WHY OR WHY NOT?

_____

_____

_____

_____

WHERE DOES THIS BELIEF COME FROM?
EVALUATE THE SOURCES TO HELP DETERMINE IF THEY HAVE ANY VALIDITY IN
YOUR LIFE TODAY.

_____

_____

_____

_____

_____

_____

HOW HAS THIS BELIEF AFFECTED YOUR LIFE UP UNTIL NOW? WHAT HAS THIS BELIEF PREVENTED YOU FROM DOING?

HOW WOULD YOUR LIFE CHANGE IF YOU ELIMINATED THIS BELIEF?

_____

_____

_____

_____

_____

_____

_____

WHAT POSITIVE BELIEFS WOULD BE BETTER FOR HELPING YOU ATTAIN YOUR GOALS? CREATE A NEW EMPOWERING TRUTH USING THESE POSITIVE BELIEFS.

_____

_____

_____

_____

_____

_____

WHAT EVIDENCE SUPPORTS THIS NEW TRUTH? HOW DOES THIS NEW TRUTH MAKE YOU FEEL?

_____

_____

_____

_____

_____

_____

IF YOU ADOPTED THIS NEW BELIEF AND APPLIED IT TO YOUR
LIFE, WHAT WOULD BE DIFFERENT IN YOUR LIFE?

NEW TRUTHS

Studies show there is power in putting pen to paper — writing something down can make it more real. On the following pages, rewrite your new empowering truths created in the previous step into an affirmation you can say to yourself daily.

An affirmation is a positive statement you say often and consistently with emotion as if it were already happening. It is a powerful way to program your mind to believe that the new empowering truth is already true. The more you say it, the more you will experience it as reality.

Affirmations are powerful because they create a vibrational frequency that attracts what you say. They change your mindset from negative to positive and help you see the world differently. The purpose of an affirmation is to create change by programming your subconscious mind with new beliefs. It's not enough to just think about what you want but also focus on how it feels.

Let's say, for example, that your new empowering truth is: "I am a successful business owner," and you want to create an affirmation. Try saying something like: "I am attracting clients and building relationships that will help me reach my goals." This affirmation is more powerful because it's specific to the desired outcome of being a successful business owner. In this example, the statement "I am attracting clients and building relationships that will help me reach my goals" tells your subconscious mind what

you want to achieve. It also suggests that taking action —
attracting clients and building relationships—will help
you achieve your goals.

Affirmations are most effective when written in the
present tense as if they were happening right now, even
though you may not be experiencing them yet. Because
the subconscious mind does not differentiate between
past, present, and future, it only understands what is
happening in the present moment.

Affirmations work because they train your subconscious
mind to believe what you say is true. As a result, you
begin to see evidence of the affirmation in your life.

MY NEW TRUTHS

_____

_____

_____

_____

_____

_____

_____

_____

_____

_____

_____

_____

_____

_____

_____

_____

_____

_____

_____

_____

_____

_____

_____

_____

_____

_____

_____

_____

MY NEW TRUTHS

_____
_____
_____
_____
_____
_____
_____
_____
_____
_____
_____
_____
_____
_____
_____
_____
_____
_____
_____
_____
_____
_____
_____
_____
_____

MY NEW TRUTHS

MY NEW TRUTHS

Congratulations!!!

You have taken the first steps in overcoming your limiting beliefs. You have identified your limiting beliefs, challenged them, and created NEW EMPOWERING TRUTHS about each limiting belief.

Now comes the practice of remaining connected to your new empowering truths.

Part 3

START THINKING
DIFFERENTLY

CHECK YOUR THOUGHTS

Over the next 30 days, track and reflect on any new or recurring limiting beliefs that arise throughout your day. The belief can be anything from "I'm not good enough" to "I'll never find my soulmate."

Each day you notice a limiting belief invading your thoughts, take the time to write down what they are and how they show up in your thinking and behavior. Then reflect on it and use the Six Rs to Ridding Limiting Beliefs process to dismantle it. Remember that limiting beliefs are often subconscious thoughts, so the more you practice looking for them, the easier it will be to identify them.

This exercise is essential because it will help you identify patterns you have developed. We all have patterns regarding how we think and feel about ourselves, so recognizing those patterns will help you understand yourself better so you can make the necessary changes.

TODAY I HAD THE FOLLOWING LIMITING BELIEFS:

_____
_____
_____
_____
_____
_____
_____
_____

I KNOW THESE BELIEFS ARE NOT TRUE BECAUSE:

_____
_____
_____
_____
_____
_____
_____
_____

THIS IS HOW I TURNED IT AROUND:

_____
_____
_____
_____
_____
_____
_____
_____

REFLECTION

HOW DO YOU FEEL TODAY? WHAT HAVE YOUR LEARNED ABOUT
YOURSELF SINCE YESTERDAY? WHAT PROGRESS HAVE YOU
MADE?

_____

_____

_____

_____

_____

_____

_____

_____

_____

_____

_____

_____

_____

_____

_____

_____

_____

_____

_____

_____

_____

_____

_____

_____

Date: / /

TODAY I HAD THE FOLLOWING LIMITING BELIEFS:

_____
_____
_____
_____
_____
_____
_____
_____

I KNOW THESE BELIEFS ARE NOT TRUE BECAUSE:

_____
_____
_____
_____
_____
_____
_____
_____

THIS IS HOW I TURNED IT AROUND:

_____
_____
_____
_____
_____
_____
_____
_____

REFLECTION

HOW DO YOU FEEL TODAY? WHAT HAVE YOUR LEARNED ABOUT YOURSELF SINCE YESTERDAY? WHAT PROGRESS HAVE YOU MADE?

TODAY I HAD THE FOLLOWING LIMITING BELIEFS:

_____

_____

_____

_____

_____

_____

_____

_____

I KNOW THESE BELIEFS ARE NOT TRUE BECAUSE:

_____

_____

_____

_____

_____

_____

_____

_____

THIS IS HOW I TURNED IT AROUND:

_____

_____

_____

_____

_____

_____

_____

_____

REFLECTION

HOW DO YOU FEEL TODAY? WHAT HAVE YOUR LEARNED ABOUT YOURSELF SINCE YESTERDAY? WHAT PROGRESS HAVE YOU MADE?

TODAY I HAD THE FOLLOWING LIMITING BELIEFS:

_____
_____
_____
_____
_____
_____
_____
_____

I KNOW THESE BELIEFS ARE NOT TRUE BECAUSE:

_____
_____
_____
_____
_____
_____
_____
_____

THIS IS HOW I TURNED IT AROUND:

_____
_____
_____
_____
_____
_____
_____
_____

REFLECTION

HOW DO YOU FEEL TODAY? WHAT HAVE YOUR LEARNED ABOUT
YOURSELF SINCE YESTERDAY? WHAT PROGRESS HAVE YOU
MADE?

TODAY I HAD THE FOLLOWING LIMITING BELIEFS:

_____

_____

_____

_____

_____

_____

_____

I KNOW THESE BELIEFS ARE NOT TRUE BECAUSE:

_____

_____

_____

_____

_____

_____

_____

THIS IS HOW I TURNED IT AROUND:

_____

_____

_____

_____

_____

_____

_____

REFLECTION

HOW DO YOU FEEL TODAY? WHAT HAVE YOUR LEARNED ABOUT YOURSELF SINCE YESTERDAY? WHAT PROGRESS HAVE YOU MADE?

_____

_____

_____

_____

_____

_____

_____

_____

_____

_____

_____

_____

_____

_____

_____

_____

_____

_____

_____

_____

_____

TODAY I HAD THE FOLLOWING LIMITING BELIEFS:

_____

_____

_____

_____

_____

_____

_____

_____

I KNOW THESE BELIEFS ARE NOT TRUE BECAUSE:

_____

_____

_____

_____

_____

_____

_____

_____

THIS IS HOW I TURNED IT AROUND:

_____

_____

_____

_____

_____

_____

_____

_____

REFLECTION

HOW DO YOU FEEL TODAY? WHAT HAVE YOUR LEARNED ABOUT YOURSELF SINCE YESTERDAY? WHAT PROGRESS HAVE YOU MADE?

_____

_____

_____

_____

_____

_____

_____

_____

_____

_____

_____

_____

_____

_____

_____

_____

_____

_____

_____

_____

_____

TODAY I HAD THE FOLLOWING LIMITING BELIEFS:

_____

_____

_____

_____

_____

_____

_____

I KNOW THESE BELIEFS ARE NOT TRUE BECAUSE:

_____

_____

_____

_____

_____

_____

_____

THIS IS HOW I TURNED IT AROUND:

_____

_____

_____

_____

_____

_____

_____

REFLECTION

HOW DO YOU FEEL TODAY? WHAT HAVE YOUR LEARNED ABOUT YOURSELF SINCE YESTERDAY? WHAT PROGRESS HAVE YOU MADE?

_____

_____

_____

_____

_____

_____

_____

_____

_____

_____

_____

_____

_____

_____

_____

_____

_____

_____

_____

_____

_____

_____

TODAY I HAD THE FOLLOWING LIMITING BELIEFS:

_____

_____

_____

_____

_____

_____

_____

I KNOW THESE BELIEFS ARE NOT TRUE BECAUSE:

_____

_____

_____

_____

_____

_____

_____

THIS IS HOW I TURNED IT AROUND:

_____

_____

_____

_____

_____

_____

_____

REFLECTION

HOW DO YOU FEEL TODAY? WHAT HAVE YOUR LEARNED ABOUT YOURSELF SINCE YESTERDAY? WHAT PROGRESS HAVE YOU MADE?

_____

_____

_____

_____

_____

_____

_____

_____

_____

_____

_____

_____

_____

_____

_____

_____

_____

_____

_____

_____

_____

TODAY I HAD THE FOLLOWING LIMITING BELIEFS:

_____
_____
_____
_____
_____
_____
_____
_____

I KNOW THESE BELIEFS ARE NOT TRUE BECAUSE:

_____
_____
_____
_____
_____
_____
_____
_____

THIS IS HOW I TURNED IT AROUND:

_____
_____
_____
_____
_____
_____
_____
_____

REFLECTION

HOW DO YOU FEEL TODAY? WHAT HAVE YOUR LEARNED ABOUT YOURSELF SINCE YESTERDAY? WHAT PROGRESS HAVE YOU MADE?

TODAY I HAD THE FOLLOWING LIMITING BELIEFS:

_____

_____

_____

_____

_____

_____

_____

I KNOW THESE BELIEFS ARE NOT TRUE BECAUSE:

_____

_____

_____

_____

_____

_____

_____

THIS IS HOW I TURNED IT AROUND:

_____

_____

_____

_____

_____

_____

_____

REFLECTION

HOW DO YOU FEEL TODAY? WHAT HAVE YOUR LEARNED ABOUT YOURSELF SINCE YESTERDAY? WHAT PROGRESS HAVE YOU MADE?

TODAY I HAD THE FOLLOWING LIMITING BELIEFS:

_____
_____
_____
_____
_____
_____
_____
_____

I KNOW THESE BELIEFS ARE NOT TRUE BECAUSE:

_____
_____
_____
_____
_____
_____
_____
_____

THIS IS HOW I TURNED IT AROUND:

_____
_____
_____
_____
_____
_____
_____
_____

REFLECTION

HOW DO YOU FEEL TODAY? WHAT HAVE YOUR LEARNED ABOUT
YOURSELF SINCE YESTERDAY? WHAT PROGRESS HAVE YOU
MADE?

TODAY I HAD THE FOLLOWING LIMITING BELIEFS:

_____
_____
_____
_____
_____
_____
_____
_____

I KNOW THESE BELIEFS ARE NOT TRUE BECAUSE:

_____
_____
_____
_____
_____
_____
_____
_____

THIS IS HOW I TURNED IT AROUND:

_____
_____
_____
_____
_____
_____
_____

REFLECTION

HOW DO YOU FEEL TODAY? WHAT HAVE YOUR LEARNED ABOUT YOURSELF SINCE YESTERDAY? WHAT PROGRESS HAVE YOU MADE?

TODAY I HAD THE FOLLOWING LIMITING BELIEFS:

_____
_____
_____
_____
_____
_____
_____
_____

I KNOW THESE BELIEFS ARE NOT TRUE BECAUSE:

_____
_____
_____
_____
_____
_____
_____
_____

THIS IS HOW I TURNED IT AROUND:

_____
_____
_____
_____
_____
_____
_____

REFLECTION

HOW DO YOU FEEL TODAY? WHAT HAVE YOUR LEARNED ABOUT YOURSELF SINCE YESTERDAY? WHAT PROGRESS HAVE YOU MADE?

_____

_____

_____

_____

_____

_____

_____

_____

_____

_____

_____

_____

_____

_____

_____

_____

_____

_____

_____

_____

_____

_____

_____

_____

TODAY I HAD THE FOLLOWING LIMITING BELIEFS:

_____

_____

_____

_____

_____

_____

_____

_____

I KNOW THESE BELIEFS ARE NOT TRUE BECAUSE:

_____

_____

_____

_____

_____

_____

_____

_____

THIS IS HOW I TURNED IT AROUND:

_____

_____

_____

_____

_____

_____

_____

_____

REFLECTION

HOW DO YOU FEEL TODAY? WHAT HAVE YOUR LEARNED ABOUT
YOURSELF SINCE YESTERDAY? WHAT PROGRESS HAVE YOU
MADE?

_____

_____

_____

_____

_____

_____

_____

_____

_____

_____

_____

_____

_____

_____

_____

_____

_____

_____

_____

_____

_____

_____

TODAY I HAD THE FOLLOWING LIMITING BELIEFS:

_____

_____

_____

_____

_____

_____

_____

_____

I KNOW THESE BELIEFS ARE NOT TRUE BECAUSE:

_____

_____

_____

_____

_____

_____

_____

_____

THIS IS HOW I TURNED IT AROUND:

_____

_____

_____

_____

_____

_____

_____

_____

REFLECTION

HOW DO YOU FEEL TODAY? WHAT HAVE YOUR LEARNED ABOUT YOURSELF SINCE YESTERDAY? WHAT PROGRESS HAVE YOU MADE?

_____

_____

_____

_____

_____

_____

_____

_____

_____

_____

_____

_____

_____

_____

_____

_____

_____

_____

_____

_____

_____

_____

_____

TODAY I HAD THE FOLLOWING LIMITING BELIEFS:

_____
_____
_____
_____
_____
_____
_____
_____

I KNOW THESE BELIEFS ARE NOT TRUE BECAUSE:

_____
_____
_____
_____
_____
_____
_____
_____

THIS IS HOW I TURNED IT AROUND:

_____
_____
_____
_____
_____
_____
_____
_____

REFLECTION

HOW DO YOU FEEL TODAY? WHAT HAVE YOUR LEARNED ABOUT YOURSELF SINCE YESTERDAY? WHAT PROGRESS HAVE YOU MADE?

_____

_____

_____

_____

_____

_____

_____

_____

_____

_____

_____

_____

_____

_____

_____

_____

_____

_____

_____

_____

_____

_____

_____

TODAY I HAD THE FOLLOWING LIMITING BELIEFS:

_____

_____

_____

_____

_____

_____

_____

_____

I KNOW THESE BELIEFS ARE NOT TRUE BECAUSE:

_____

_____

_____

_____

_____

_____

_____

_____

THIS IS HOW I TURNED IT AROUND:

_____

_____

_____

_____

_____

_____

_____

_____

REFLECTION

HOW DO YOU FEEL TODAY? WHAT HAVE YOUR LEARNED ABOUT YOURSELF SINCE YESTERDAY? WHAT PROGRESS HAVE YOU MADE?

TODAY I HAD THE FOLLOWING LIMITING BELIEFS:

_____

_____

_____

_____

_____

_____

_____

I KNOW THESE BELIEFS ARE NOT TRUE BECAUSE:

_____

_____

_____

_____

_____

_____

_____

THIS IS HOW I TURNED IT AROUND:

_____

_____

_____

_____

_____

_____

_____

REFLECTION

HOW DO YOU FEEL TODAY? WHAT HAVE YOUR LEARNED ABOUT
YOURSELF SINCE YESTERDAY? WHAT PROGRESS HAVE YOU
MADE?

_____

_____

_____

_____

_____

_____

_____

_____

_____

_____

_____

_____

_____

_____

_____

_____

_____

_____

_____

_____

_____

TODAY I HAD THE FOLLOWING LIMITING BELIEFS:

_____

_____

_____

_____

_____

_____

_____

I KNOW THESE BELIEFS ARE NOT TRUE BECAUSE:

_____

_____

_____

_____

_____

_____

_____

THIS IS HOW I TURNED IT AROUND:

_____

_____

_____

_____

_____

_____

REFLECTION

HOW DO YOU FEEL TODAY? WHAT HAVE YOUR LEARNED ABOUT YOURSELF SINCE YESTERDAY? WHAT PROGRESS HAVE YOU MADE?

_____

_____

_____

_____

_____

_____

_____

_____

_____

_____

_____

_____

_____

_____

_____

_____

_____

_____

_____

_____

_____

_____

_____

TODAY I HAD THE FOLLOWING LIMITING BELIEFS:

_____

_____

_____

_____

_____

_____

_____

I KNOW THESE BELIEFS ARE NOT TRUE BECAUSE:

_____

_____

_____

_____

_____

_____

_____

THIS IS HOW I TURNED IT AROUND:

_____

_____

_____

_____

_____

_____

_____

REFLECTION

HOW DO YOU FEEL TODAY? WHAT HAVE YOUR LEARNED ABOUT
YOURSELF SINCE YESTERDAY? WHAT PROGRESS HAVE YOU
MADE?

_____

_____

_____

_____

_____

_____

_____

_____

_____

_____

_____

_____

_____

_____

_____

_____

_____

_____

_____

_____

_____

TODAY I HAD THE FOLLOWING LIMITING BELIEFS:

_____

_____

_____

_____

_____

_____

_____

I KNOW THESE BELIEFS ARE NOT TRUE BECAUSE:

_____

_____

_____

_____

_____

_____

_____

THIS IS HOW I TURNED IT AROUND:

_____

_____

_____

_____

_____

_____

_____

_____

REFLECTION

HOW DO YOU FEEL TODAY? WHAT HAVE YOUR LEARNED ABOUT YOURSELF SINCE YESTERDAY? WHAT PROGRESS HAVE YOU MADE?

_____

_____

_____

_____

_____

_____

_____

_____

_____

_____

_____

_____

_____

_____

_____

_____

_____

_____

_____

_____

_____

TODAY I HAD THE FOLLOWING LIMITING BELIEFS:

_____

_____

_____

_____

_____

_____

_____

I KNOW THESE BELIEFS ARE NOT TRUE BECAUSE:

_____

_____

_____

_____

_____

_____

_____

THIS IS HOW I TURNED IT AROUND:

_____

_____

_____

_____

_____

_____

_____

REFLECTION

HOW DO YOU FEEL TODAY? WHAT HAVE YOUR LEARNED ABOUT YOURSELF SINCE YESTERDAY? WHAT PROGRESS HAVE YOU MADE?

Date: / /

TODAY I HAD THE FOLLOWING LIMITING BELIEFS:

_____
_____
_____
_____
_____
_____
_____
_____

I KNOW THESE BELIEFS ARE NOT TRUE BECAUSE:

_____
_____
_____
_____
_____
_____
_____
_____

THIS IS HOW I TURNED IT AROUND:

_____
_____
_____
_____
_____
_____
_____
_____

REFLECTION

HOW DO YOU FEEL TODAY? WHAT HAVE YOUR LEARNED ABOUT
YOURSELF SINCE YESTERDAY? WHAT PROGRESS HAVE YOU
MADE?

TODAY I HAD THE FOLLOWING LIMITING BELIEFS:

_____
_____
_____
_____
_____
_____
_____
_____

I KNOW THESE BELIEFS ARE NOT TRUE BECAUSE:

_____
_____
_____
_____
_____
_____
_____
_____

THIS IS HOW I TURNED IT AROUND:

_____
_____
_____
_____
_____
_____
_____
_____

REFLECTION

HOW DO YOU FEEL TODAY? WHAT HAVE YOUR LEARNED ABOUT
YOURSELF SINCE YESTERDAY? WHAT PROGRESS HAVE YOU
MADE?

_____

_____

_____

_____

_____

_____

_____

_____

_____

_____

_____

_____

_____

_____

_____

_____

_____

_____

_____

_____

_____

_____

TODAY I HAD THE FOLLOWING LIMITING BELIEFS:

_____

_____

_____

_____

_____

_____

_____

I KNOW THESE BELIEFS ARE NOT TRUE BECAUSE:

_____

_____

_____

_____

_____

_____

_____

THIS IS HOW I TURNED IT AROUND:

_____

_____

_____

_____

_____

_____

_____

REFLECTION

HOW DO YOU FEEL TODAY? WHAT HAVE YOUR LEARNED ABOUT
YOURSELF SINCE YESTERDAY? WHAT PROGRESS HAVE YOU
MADE?

TODAY I HAD THE FOLLOWING LIMITING BELIEFS:

_____

_____

_____

_____

_____

_____

_____

_____

I KNOW THESE BELIEFS ARE NOT TRUE BECAUSE:

_____

_____

_____

_____

_____

_____

_____

_____

THIS IS HOW I TURNED IT AROUND:

_____

_____

_____

_____

_____

_____

_____

REFLECTION

HOW DO YOU FEEL TODAY? WHAT HAVE YOUR LEARNED ABOUT
YOURSELF SINCE YESTERDAY? WHAT PROGRESS HAVE YOU
MADE?

TODAY I HAD THE FOLLOWING LIMITING BELIEFS:

_____

_____

_____

_____

_____

_____

_____

_____

I KNOW THESE BELIEFS ARE NOT TRUE BECAUSE:

_____

_____

_____

_____

_____

_____

_____

_____

THIS IS HOW I TURNED IT AROUND:

_____

_____

_____

_____

_____

_____

_____

_____

REFLECTION

HOW DO YOU FEEL TODAY? WHAT HAVE YOUR LEARNED ABOUT YOURSELF SINCE YESTERDAY? WHAT PROGRESS HAVE YOU MADE?

_____

_____

_____

_____

_____

_____

_____

_____

_____

_____

_____

_____

_____

_____

_____

_____

_____

_____

_____

_____

_____

TODAY I HAD THE FOLLOWING LIMITING BELIEFS:

_____
_____
_____
_____
_____
_____
_____
_____

I KNOW THESE BELIEFS ARE NOT TRUE BECAUSE:

_____
_____
_____
_____
_____
_____
_____
_____

THIS IS HOW I TURNED IT AROUND:

_____
_____
_____
_____
_____
_____
_____
_____

REFLECTION

HOW DO YOU FEEL TODAY? WHAT HAVE YOUR LEARNED ABOUT
YOURSELF SINCE YESTERDAY? WHAT PROGRESS HAVE YOU
MADE?

_____

_____

_____

_____

_____

_____

_____

_____

_____

_____

_____

_____

_____

_____

_____

_____

_____

_____

_____

_____

_____

_____

TODAY I HAD THE FOLLOWING LIMITING BELIEFS:

_____
_____
_____
_____
_____
_____
_____
_____

I KNOW THESE BELIEFS ARE NOT TRUE BECAUSE:

_____
_____
_____
_____
_____
_____
_____
_____
_____

THIS IS HOW I TURNED IT AROUND:

_____
_____
_____
_____
_____
_____
_____

REFLECTION

HOW DO YOU FEEL TODAY? WHAT HAVE YOUR LEARNED ABOUT
YOURSELF SINCE YESTERDAY? WHAT PROGRESS HAVE YOU
MADE?

_____

_____

_____

_____

_____

_____

_____

_____

_____

_____

_____

_____

_____

_____

_____

_____

_____

_____

_____

_____

_____

_____

TODAY I HAD THE FOLLOWING LIMITING BELIEFS:

_____

_____

_____

_____

_____

_____

_____

_____

I KNOW THESE BELIEFS ARE NOT TRUE BECAUSE:

_____

_____

_____

_____

_____

_____

_____

_____

THIS IS HOW I TURNED IT AROUND:

_____

_____

_____

_____

_____

_____

_____

_____

REFLECTION

HOW DO YOU FEEL TODAY? WHAT HAVE YOUR LEARNED ABOUT
YOURSELF SINCE YESTERDAY? WHAT PROGRESS HAVE YOU
MADE?

_____

_____

_____

_____

_____

_____

_____

_____

_____

_____

_____

_____

_____

_____

_____

_____

_____

_____

_____

_____

_____

Part 4

START CELEBRATING
YOUR PROGRESS

TRACK YOUR PROGRESS

As you overcome a limiting belief, track your progress. Tracking your progress will help you to celebrate your wins, keep yourself motivated, notice your successes and keep going when you face setbacks. It's okay to have setbacks but don't let them derail you for too long.

To track your progress, ask yourself these questions:
- What was the belief?
- When did I start working on it?
- How has my thinking changed?
- What have been my successes?
- What challenges have I faced?
- How have I handled them?
- What has been the result of my efforts?

Remember, change is a process, not an event. Celebrate each step along the way!

LIST A LIMITING BELIEF THAT YOU HAD BUT **NO LONGER** BELIEVE.

_____

_____

_____

_____

_____

_____

_____

_____

_____

_____

HOW DID THIS BELIEF PREVIOUSLY AFFECT YOUR SUCCESS? HOW IS YOUR LIFE DIFFERENT NOW THAT YOU NO LONGER BELIEVE THIS?

_____

_____

_____

_____

_____

_____

_____

_____

_____

LIST A LIMITING BELIEF THAT YOU HAD BUT **NO LONGER** BELIEVE.

_____

_____

_____

_____

_____

_____

_____

_____

_____

_____

HOW DID THIS BELIEF PREVIOUSLY AFFECT YOUR SUCCESS? HOW IS YOUR LIFE DIFFERENT NOW THAT YOU NO LONGER BELIEVE THIS?

_____

_____

_____

_____

_____

_____

_____

_____

_____

LIST A LIMITING BELIEF THAT YOU HAD BUT **NO LONGER**
BELIEVE.

_____

_____

_____

_____

_____

_____

_____

_____

_____

_____

HOW DID THIS BELIEF PREVIOUSLY AFFECT YOUR SUCCESS?
HOW IS YOUR LIFE DIFFERENT NOW THAT YOU NO LONGER
BELIEVE THIS?

_____

_____

_____

_____

_____

_____

_____

_____

_____

_____

LIST A LIMITING BELIEF THAT YOU HAD BUT **NO LONGER** BELIEVE.

_____

_____

_____

_____

_____

_____

_____

_____

_____

_____

HOW DID THIS BELIEF PREVIOUSLY AFFECT YOUR SUCCESS? HOW IS YOUR LIFE DIFFERENT NOW THAT YOU NO LONGER BELIEVE THIS?

_____

_____

_____

_____

_____

_____

_____

_____

_____

LIST A LIMITING BELIEF THAT YOU HAD BUT **NO LONGER** BELIEVE.

_____

_____

_____

_____

_____

_____

_____

_____

_____

_____

HOW DID THIS BELIEF PREVIOUSLY AFFECT YOUR SUCCESS? HOW IS YOUR LIFE DIFFERENT NOW THAT YOU NO LONGER BELIEVE THIS?

_____

_____

_____

_____

_____

_____

_____

_____

LIST A LIMITING BELIEF THAT YOU HAD BUT **NO LONGER** BELIEVE.

_____

_____

_____

_____

_____

_____

_____

_____

_____

HOW DID THIS BELIEF PREVIOUSLY AFFECT YOUR SUCCESS? HOW IS YOUR LIFE DIFFERENT NOW THAT YOU NO LONGER BELIEVE THIS?

_____

_____

_____

_____

_____

_____

_____

_____

LIST A LIMITING BELIEF THAT YOU HAD BUT **NO LONGER** BELIEVE.

_____

_____

_____

_____

_____

_____

_____

_____

_____

HOW DID THIS BELIEF PREVIOUSLY AFFECT YOUR SUCCESS? HOW IS YOUR LIFE DIFFERENT NOW THAT YOU NO LONGER BELIEVE THIS?

_____

_____

_____

_____

_____

_____

_____

_____

LIST A LIMITING BELIEF THAT YOU HAD BUT **NO LONGER** BELIEVE.

_____

_____

_____

_____

_____

_____

_____

_____

_____

_____

HOW DID THIS BELIEF PREVIOUSLY AFFECT YOUR SUCCESS? HOW IS YOUR LIFE DIFFERENT NOW THAT YOU NO LONGER BELIEVE THIS?

_____

_____

_____

_____

_____

_____

_____

_____

_____

LIST A LIMITING BELIEF THAT YOU HAD BUT **NO LONGER** BELIEVE.

_____

_____

_____

_____

_____

_____

_____

_____

_____

_____

HOW DID THIS BELIEF PREVIOUSLY AFFECT YOUR SUCCESS? HOW IS YOUR LIFE DIFFERENT NOW THAT YOU NO LONGER BELIEVE THIS?

_____

_____

_____

_____

_____

_____

_____

_____

_____

LIST A LIMITING BELIEF THAT YOU HAD BUT **NO LONGER** BELIEVE.

_____

_____

_____

_____

_____

_____

_____

_____

_____

_____

HOW DID THIS BELIEF PREVIOUSLY AFFECT YOUR SUCCESS? HOW IS YOUR LIFE DIFFERENT NOW THAT YOU NO LONGER BELIEVE THIS?

_____

_____

_____

_____

_____

_____

_____

_____

_____

Bonus

30 POSITIVE AFFIRMATIONS FOR A BETTER YOU

30 POSITIVE AFFIRMATIONS FOR A BETTER YOU

1. I am starting a positive new stage in my life.
2. I am a beautiful work in progress.
3. I am mentally strong and stable.
4. I am doing the best that I can, and that's all I ask of myself.
5. I am proud of who I am.
6. I am I choosing to see the light that I am in this world.
7. I am grateful for the ability to learn and grow.
8. I am passionate about constantly being better.
9. I am making myself better and refusing to dwell on the mistakes of the past.
10. I am in charge of my life story.
11. I am confident in my ability to achieve success.
12. I am on a path to achieving my dreams.
13. I am creating a firm foundation for success.
14. I am successful in all that I do.
15. I am built to survive any challenge that comes my way.
16. I am doing my best, and that is always enough.
17. I am ready to become the best version of myself.
18. I am focusing on the positives and allow the negatives to slide by.
19. I'm surrounded by the energy of calm, peace, and positivity.
20. I am a loving, faithful, respectful, and loyal person.
21. I am lovable, likable, and unforgettable.
22. I am attracting someone who realizes how amazing I am.
23. I am at peace. I am confident. I am secure.
24. I am calm, confident, and powerful.
25. I am too amazing to worry about being perfect.
26. I am not trapped or stuck, and everything is always changing.
27. I am allowed to release old thought patterns that no longer serve me.
28. I am worthy of accomplishment, success, and abundance.
29. I am receiving an infinite supply of financial energy from within.
30. I am intelligent enough to receive wealth and prosperity.

ABOUT THE AUTHOR

Harriet M. Harris, MBA, known as The Limitless Business Coach, is a mom, wife, and an entrepreneur who helps ambitious women live a life without limits by helping them remove internal roadblocks so they can FINALLY create the life and business they have always wanted.

Harriet knows that being an ambitious woman is not always an easy journey because women are constantly faced with limitations: their own expectations, other people's expectations, society's expectations... the list goes on and on. And that's why it takes so much work to get over yourself! But it can be done—and that's what she does best.

In addition to being an experienced business owner, Harriet has assisted women with starting and growing businesses for more than a decade so she knows how to assist you with getting your business off the ground — and then helping to build the systems, processes, and accountability structures needed to make it happen.

But that's not all she does: she's also experienced in overcoming life experiences—from childhood trauma to marriage drama. She realizes that some of the biggest limitations women face today are linked to the things they've experienced throughout their lives. Identifying and overcoming her own limiting beliefs helped her evolve into a confident, bold, and happy leader & business coach who knows how to help others overcome limitations that keep them from being the best version of themselves.

Harriet's personal story is what inspired her to help others overcome their limitations. She knows from experience the value of feeling like you are finally able to move past thoughts and beliefs that have kept you stuck for what may feel like a lifetime. Harriet believes that everyone has the power within them to create their ideal life and business—it doesn't matter where they are in their journey right now or how much they've struggled in the past. It just matters that they make the decision to get started.

Harriet spent nearly two decades working in Corporate America when she decided to create a business that would allow her to fulfill her purpose—helping women who want to start businesses but don't know how. She is passionate about helping them realize their potential so they can create lives and businesses they love. Today, Harriet is an author, speaker, and coach who helps women entrepreneurs create success on their own terms.

To learn more about Harriet's course offerings, free resources or how she can help you break through the barriers that have been keeping you from the success you desire, visit her website at www.harrietmharris.com/linkinbio or email her directly at contact@harrietmharris.com.

www.ingramcontent.com/pod-product-compliance
Lightning Source LLC
Chambersburg PA
CBHW060516130626
46553CB00002B/526